MYTHOLOGY

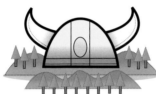
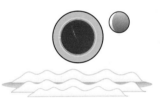

D1435070

First published 2014 by Kingfisher
an imprint of Macmillan Children's Books
a division of Macmillan Publishers Limited
20 New Wharf Road, London N1 9RR
Basingstoke and Oxford
Associated companies throughout the world
www.panmacmillan.com

ISBN: 978-0-7534-3711-7

Consultants:
Professor Richard Buxton (Greek)
Dr. John Haywood (Norse)
Dr. Aidan Johnson (Egyptian)

Designed and created by Basher www.basherbooks.com
Text written by Mary Frances Budzik

Dedicated to Blake Stanley & Family

10 9 8 7 6 5 4 3 2 1
1TR/0414/WKT/UG/128MA

A CIP catalogue record for this book is available from the British Library.

For more information, please visit www.kingfisherbooks.com

Printed in China

CONTENTS

Introduction

Welcome to the domain of some real superstars: the gods and goddesses. Today, they are just characters in stories (myths), but once upon a time people thought they were everywhere and worshipped them. Myths are found all over the world, but in this book we've got the gods and goddesses from just three cultures: ancient Greek, Norse and ancient Egyptian.

These guys certainly know how to have fun. Some of them, such as mighty Zeus, thunderous Thor and the sun god Ra, have super-cool gear – shock-and-awe thunderbolts, wicked weapons and a sky boat cooler than a private jet. Others, such as snake-haired Medusa, have magical powers that are to-die-for... quite literally, sometimes! But these dudes also offered people something to believe in when life was looking bleak. Their tall tales of great heroism in the face of betrayal and revenge provided an orderly structure on which to found lasting societies. And with their family rivalries, dirty tricks and unbounded sense of adventure, you can still rely on them today to deliver when it comes to star-quality entertainment!

Introduction

Chapter 1
Ancient Greeks

Is there anything better than the life of a Greek deity –
or a Roman one, for that matter, since they're virtually
the same (see pages 122–123)? For starters, these are
people, not animals or monsters. Secondly, with the
exception of ugly Hephaestus, they all have supermodel
good looks. And thirdly, they're immortal. That's right –
they live forever! These ancients are a mixture of civilized
and wild, just like the landscape of Greece itself. There
are tensions and rivalries between them, too. You see,
these guys just love to stick their noses into human
affairs. And the results aren't always pretty...

Zeus

 Hera

 Poseidon

 Hades

 Ares

 Hebe

 Artemis

 Apollo

 Hermes

 Athena

 Aphrodite

 Demeter

 Dionysus

 Asclepius

 Pan

 The Muses

 Hephaestus

 Heracles

 Odysseus

 Orpheus

 Medusa

 Minotaur

Zeus
■ Ancient Greeks

☀ God of gods on Mount Olympus; Zeus rhymes with 'juice'
☀ Creates disturbances in the sky – thunder and lightning
☀ The oak tree and eagle symbolize his strength

Call me Big Daddy! I am the mover and shaker on Mount Olympus – gatherer of storm clouds, hurler of thunderbolts and maker of rain. King of the gods, I also happen to be father to more than a few.

Always one to take on the tough jobs, I conquered my own dad, Cronus. That power-crazed monster was head of the old guard, the Titans. He swallowed his first five kids whole, just to make sure that they couldn't take over his throne. By the time I was born, my mother Rhea was wise to his ways and hid me in a cave. Once I'd grown up, I got my own back and tricked Cronus into sicking up my siblings. As you can imagine, they were super-grateful for the rescue. I led them against Dad in a war called the Titanomachy. We won, and now I rule Olympus.

● Zeus conquered the massive serpent Typhon using his thunderbolts
● He lent his favourite child, Athena, his shield adorned with Medusa's head
● Despite his power, Zeus had no control over the Fates
● Roman name: Jupiter

Zeus

Hera
Ancient Greeks

- ☀ Queen of Mount Olympus; Hera rhymes with 'era'
- ☀ Wife of Zeus and goddess of marriage and childbirth
- ☀ She rides in a chariot drawn by peacocks

Marriage to Zeus can be a challenge. I have been known to take a little revenge on some of my hubby's mortal girlfriends. Take Semele, for example. I persuaded her to demand that Zeus show her his full splendour. How was I to know she'd burn to a crisp at the sight of him?

Still, I like to remember the good times, such as when big, bad Zeus transformed himself into a shivering little cuckoo chick just so that I'd cuddle him. Before I knew it, we were married! The earth goddess Gaia gave me some golden apples as a wedding gift, and I made a sleepless, hundred-eyed dragon guard the orchard I planted. Patroness of marriage, I chose the peacock as my symbol. All those wide-open eyes in its tail remind a certain god that I am always watching!

- ● Angry at her interference, Zeus once dangled Hera from a cliff by her wrists
- ● Hera helped Jason win the Golden Fleece by hiding him from his enemies
- ● The Heraion, an important temple in the city of Argos, was dedicated to Hera
- ● Roman name: Juno

Hera

Poseidon
■ Ancient Greeks

☀ Brother of Zeus and Hades; Poseidon rhymes with 'Jo side-on'
☀ God of the sea and very important to the seafaring Greeks
☀ The trident and the dolphin are Poseidon's symbols

After we defeated the Titans, I drew lots with my brothers and the sea became my realm. I live in a pearl-and-coral palace, attended by sea nymphs called Nereids.

The trouble is, when I get angry (and boy, do I get angry), I strike the seabed with my three-pronged trident, creating gales, earthquakes and tsunamis. No wonder sailors try never to cross me! I can hold a grudge, too! After Odysseus blinded my one-eyed son Polyphemus, I made him wander the seas for ten years – even though I knew he'd been acting in self defence. My chariot is drawn by hippocampuses – winged seahorses that can gallop over or under the waves. God of horses, I am the father of the divine winged horse Pegasus and the immortal horse Areion, who was owned by Heracles.

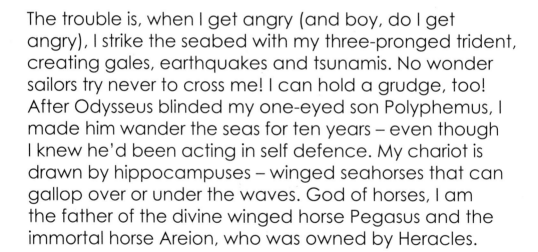

● Poseidon's wife Amphitrite was a sea nymph; their son Triton was a merman
● Athena competed against Poseidon to be patron of Athens… and won
● Poseidon's earthquakes earned him the nickname 'Earth Shaker'
● Roman name: Neptune

Poseidon

Hades
■ Ancient Greeks

☀ God of the underworld; Hades rhymes with 'say cheese'
☀ Cerberus, a three-headed dog, guards the gates to his world
☀ He abducts Demeter's daughter, Persephone, to be his wife

When my brothers Zeus, Poseidon and I drew lots, the underworld fell to me. I wasn't sent to this terrible place for committing a sin – I just won it in a game of chance!

Unlike my brothers, I seldom speak or interfere in the affairs of mortal men. I don't have to! I know that, in the end, I'll have as many permanent guests in my dark domain as I want. I simply wait for Hermes to lead them down to my cavern of shades deep beneath the earth. They'll never get out again! I own all the precious metals and gems that sparkle down here, but I never get to show off my wealth because no one ever invites me anywhere. Is it any wonder I carried off Persephone when I saw her gathering flowers? With my grim appearance, it was a safe bet that I would never find a *willing* bride!

● All riches below earth were his, but Hades owned no property above ground
● The darkest pit of his underworld, Tartarus, was reserved for evildoers
● The ancient Greeks did not build any temples to honour Hades
● Roman name: Pluto

Hades

Ares

Ancient Greeks

✳ Son of Zeus and Hera; Ares rhymes with 'fairies'
✳ The god of war, he is symbolized by the helmet and the spear
✳ His girlfriend is Aphrodite, the wife of ugly Hephaestus

With parents like mine, is it any wonder that I was born craving the battlefield? I've been called grim, murderous, rebellious, bloodthirsty and hungry for war, but no one can deny that I am bold and strong. It's me they call when they want to win at any cost.

As father of the race of Amazons, I honour female warriors. My sons Phobos (Fear) and Deimos (Terror) accompany me into battle and urge on my fire-breathing horses, while my Stymphalian birds circle overhead and fire their spear-tipped feathers. Although we make an odd couple, lovely Aphrodite cannot resist me. My blood relatives betray me, though. My own sister, Athena, and my mother, Hera, helped the Greek warrior Diomedes to wound me during the Trojan War.

● Ares was Zeus's least favourite offspring; Zeus hated Ares's love of quarrels
● Aphrodite persuaded Ares to support the Trojans during the Trojan War
● The Amazons were a race of warrior women who loved to do battle
● Roman name: Mars

Ares

Hebe
■ Ancient Greeks

☀ The goddess of youth; Hebe rhymes with 'jeebie'
☀ She is the daughter of Zeus and Hera
☀ Waitress to the Olympians, Hebe serves ambrosia and nectar

Sigh. Even on Mount Olympus, it's the kids who have to set the table. Although my own story isn't well known, I could tell plenty of tales about what happens at our family suppers! Cupbearer of the gods? *Please!* That's not an honour. I mean, you just try carrying a tray when you're dodging thunderbolts, tridents and arrows!

I am the goddess of youth. So OK, I got to marry Heracles, who's like the strongest dude ever, but I do think Mum might have guessed I'd prefer somebody a bit younger. 'Hebe dear, would you pass me that amphora?' And that's another thing – the menu on Olympus! Honey-sweet nectar and delectable ambrosia day after day. I've said over and over, why can't we have something different for dinner? Like, less sugary? But oh no!

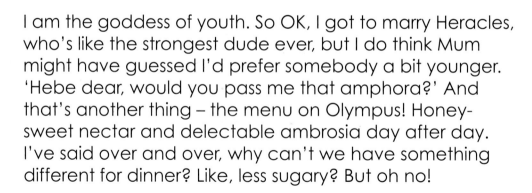

● Ambrosia (food) and nectar (drink) gave the gods their immortality
● Hebe had two sons with Heracles; they remained forever young
● A bit of a mechanic, Hebe helped Hera bolt the wheels on to her chariot!
● Roman name: Juventus

Hebe

Artemis

■ Ancient Greeks

�֍ Daughter of Zeus and Leto; Artemis rhymes with 'charter miss'
✖ Goddess of the moon and Mistress of Animals
✖ Artemis has a chariot drawn by horned deer with golden bits

Tall and nimble, I'm a fierce hunter, especially of stags. You'll know me by the bow and arrow on my back or by the beloved hounds at my side. Because my father is Zeus, jealous Hera (his wife) forced my mum to give birth to me alone on the island of Delos. Then I helped to deliver my twin, Apollo. Can you blame me for vowing there and then to remain free and single forever?

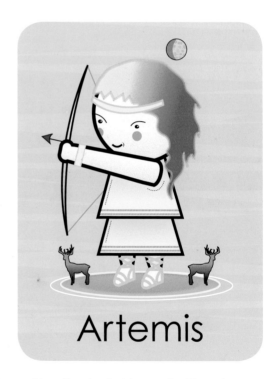

Artemis

● Artemis asked Zeus for a saffron-coloured hunting tunic trimmed with red
● Her sacred animals were the stag and the deer; the quail was her sacred bird
● Little girls dressed and danced as bears in her honour
● Roman name: Diana

Apollo
Ancient Greeks

* Son of Zeus and Leto; Apollo rhymes with 'a swallow'
* Artemis's twin brother, and the original beautiful young man
* He was born under a palm tree on the island of Delos

Apollo

I'm one handsome guy. The sun god, I am the bringer of light, creator of sweet music on my lyre and the oracle of the future. But take care, I'm also an archer of deadly accuracy and I have a savage side – cross me at your peril. When Niobe dared to mock Mum for having only two children, I arranged the deaths of Niobe's own 14 babies. Pity is not my strong point.

- Leto laboured nine days to give birth to Apollo with only Artemis there to help
- Hymns sung to Apollo were called paeans
- The famous sanctuary at Delphi was sacred to Apollo
- Roman name: Apollo

Hermes
Ancient Greeks

✳ Son of Zeus and nymph Maia; Hermes rhymes with 'her knees'
✳ He is known for stealing, cunning and bargaining
✳ His staff shows two snakes twined around a winged rod

My fellow Olympians soon realized that I was the restless type, so they put me to work as their official messenger. Lazing around Mount Olympus is not my cup of tea! To help me move fast (and look good doing it), I wear my supersonic winged sandals and helmet.

I am known as the trickster god – and I'm light-fingered as well as fleet-footed! While still a baby, I stole Apollo's cattle and bribed him to forgive me by making him a beautiful lyre out of a turtle's shell. Since I am such a fearless traveller, I also have the solemn job of leading dead souls on their dark way to the underworld. I am the patron of crossroads, borders and boundaries because, of all the gods, I'm the one who passes most easily between Olympus, Earth and Hades.

● Hermes's herald's staff was called a caduceus
● He once rescued Ares from imprisonment in a bronze vessel
● His major centre of worship was mountainous Arcadia, his birthplace
● Roman name: Mercury

Hermes

Athena
■ Ancient Greeks

✳ Daughter of Zeus and Metis; Athena rhymes with 'hyena'
✳ She is protectress and goddess of wisdom, war and crafts
✳ Feisty Athena's symbol is the owl

I gave my father the mother of all headaches when I was born. The pain got so bad that Zeus demanded his head be split open with an axe. Out I leapt, fully armed and with a shout. Old sorehead wasn't too pleased, but what did he expect? When he swallowed my pregnant mother Metis, I guess he forgot that his powerful offspring would be immortal like him, and not so easy to get rid of!

Born holding a spear, I always champion the underdog. I rescued Orestes from the Furies (a real bunch of bad girls) and helped Odysseus (what a hero!) on his journey home from the Trojan War. I'm goddess of the city and of civilization. Greece's top metropolis Athens is named after me, and the Parthenon – the most impressive Greek temple (in my opinion) – was built in my honour.

● Athena gave the olive tree to the people of Athens
● She wore a helmet and carried a spear
● Athena sometimes wore an aegis (breastplate) adorned with Medusa's head
● Roman name: Minerva

Athena

Aphrodite
Ancient Greeks

✹ Goddess of love; Aphrodite rhymes with 'mighty'
✹ She is also goddess of beauty and has ivory-white skin
✹ Along with Ares, she is a parent of Eros, the god of love

The ultimate surfer girl, I was born out of the sea foam on the island of Cythera. Riding a scallop shell, I caught a wave to shore – my jaw-dropping beauty made quite an impression when I hit the beach. Gentle winds then carried me to Cyprus, where the Seasons dressed me in robes perfumed by roses, lilies and violets.

Would you believe that Zeus chose ugly Hephaestus as my husband? What an odd couple we make! Still, he is good at fixing things and he made my embroidered magic belt that makes anyone who wears it the most popular girl in town. Hera always wants to borrow it! And I may be vain, but I can be brave, too. I was wounded on the wrist with a spear when I shielded my son Aeneas (the founder of Rome, I must brag) during the Trojan War.

● The *Venus de Milo*, a very famous Greek statue, depicts Aphrodite
● A beauty contest won by Aphrodite set the Trojan War in motion
● Roses and myrtles were her sacred plants; doves and swans her sacred birds
● Roman name: Venus

Aphrodite

Demeter
Ancient Greeks

✳ Zeus's sister; Demeter rhymes with 'repeater'
✳ She is goddess of the harvest; sometimes called Earth Mother
✳ Demeter wears a wreath woven from ripe ears of grain

Call me the corniest goddess, I won't mind. After all, my name does mean 'grain mother'. I'm one of the oldest Olympians, yet I don't spend much time up there.

Instead, I wander the fields on earth, checking on the harvest. I taught people how to plough the ground and sow and reap grain – skills that transformed them from wandering hunter-gatherers to farmers. I look after the cycle of the seasons (from barren winter to fertile summer), so I also symbolize death and rebirth. I am a devoted mother to Persephone. When Hades abducted my daughter and took her to the underworld, I spent months searching for her. My sorrow at her loss makes the plants wither in autumn – my joy when she returns each spring makes everything green again.

● Triptolemus, the first man to grow corn, was Demeter's protégé
● The poppy was sacred to Demeter because it grew in cornfields
● The Eleusinian Mysteries were rituals held in her honour
● Roman name: Ceres

Demeter

Dionysus
■ Ancient Greeks

✹ God of winemaking; Dionysus rhymes with 'lion dice us'
✹ He is the only Olympian god to have a mortal parent
✹ Dionysus is often pictured wearing an animal skin

For a god, I've been through a lot. I was born out of a thigh – my dad Zeus's, to be exact. He had sewn me up in there for safe keeping after my mother Semele was unfortunately fried by his thunder and lightning.

My next ordeal was being torn to shreds by Titans set on me by (who else?) Hera. My grandmother Rhea had me put together again and raised by nymphs. Annoyed, Hera afflicted me with insanity, and I set off on a crazy journey to the East where I was kidnapped by pirates! I got out of *that* mess by tangling the ship's rigging in vines and flooding the decks with wine. Yep, by then I knew I was a god and that growing grapes was my destiny. Now I travel the countryside teaching men to cultivate grapevines. On a festive note, I am also the god of theatre.

● Famous Greek playwrights wrote plays for Dionysus's yearly drama festivals
● Unlike most male gods, he was not portrayed as muscular and masculine
● He was the only Olympian god whose worship promoted chaos instead of order
● Roman name: Bacchus

Dionysus

Asclepius
Ancient Greeks

* ☀ God of medicine; Asclepius rhymes with 'a sleepy puss'
* ☀ He is usually shown as a bearded older man holding a staff
* ☀ Asclepius joins Jason on his quest for the Golden Fleece

Maybe it's because my own story is so painful to recall that I've devoted my life to healing the hurts of others. My father Apollo feared that my mortal mother, Koronis, had been unfaithful, so he had Artemis slay her with an arrow. At her funeral, suddenly sorry, he cut me from her womb (my name means 'to cut open').

Apollo brought me to Chiron to raise. What a stroke of luck! This wise centaur (that's half-man, half-horse to you) was caring and gentle. In his remote cave on Mount Pelion, Chiron taught me the arts of medicinal herbs and surgery. I learned that my abilities could be used to heal rich and poor. I grew so skilled that I even raised people from the dead. And for that act of hubris, Zeus killed me with a thunderbolt!

* ● Asclepius was the father of Hygieia, the goddess of health
* ● His staff, entwined with a serpent, is a well-known symbol of medicine
* ● Serpents were said to be able to recognize healing herbs
* ● Roman name: Aesculapius

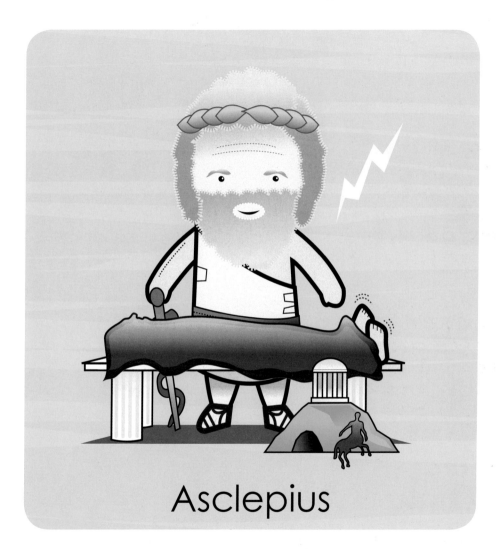

Asclepius

Pan
Ancient Greeks

* God of nature; Pan rhymes with 'man'
* Pan is also god of folk music, symbolized by his pan pipes
* A demigod (a god with one divine and one mortal parent)

I don't live on Olympus, and I'm not on Hera's radar. That's the way I like it! Let the Olympians worry about their responsibilities. All I have to do is play.

I'm a homely goat god, born with horns and hooves – all the better to caper through the groves that make up my forest home in the mountains of Arcadia. It's one of the wildest parts of ancient Greece. If you've ever walked along a shady, wooded path and felt like you were being watched, you've probably sensed my presence, hidden in a thicket, smiling naughtily. Lovely Syrinx, a nymph, turned herself into a reed to escape my pursuit. The music I heard when the wind blew through the reeds around her was so sweet that I cut them to make my pan pipes. Listen carefully and you may hear it, too!

● The harmonica is a modern version of pan pipes
● Pan's earliest shrines were often in isolated caves, rather than temples
● The 'pan' in panic is associated with him and a fear of being alone in the woods
● Roman name: Faunus

Pan

The Muses
■ Ancient Greeks

☀ Daughters of Zeus and Mnemosyne; Muses rhymes with 'fuses'
☀ They are goddesses of inspiration in the arts and sciences
☀ Each has an emblem that represents her role

Thank Zeus (our dear, naughty dad) that there are nine of us sisters in this family. Our mum had some gift for names! Here's the roll-call: Calliope, Clio, Euterpe, Melpomene, Terpsichore, Erato, Polyhymnia, Urania and Thalia.

With temperamental poets, dancers and even head-in-the-clouds astronomers invoking us 24/7, there's hardly time to frolic in a sylvan grove. Those images you see of us linking hands and dancing in pastoral delight are pure fiction (which is not one of our areas of expertise, by the way – we specialize in poetry, not prose). Our pagers beep non-stop, calling Calliope to an epic poet in need of a prologue or Terpsichore to a modern dancer in despair over a pulled tendon. You see, coddling creativity in all its forms is our job and we take it seriously.

● The Muses inspired: epic poetry (Calliope); history (Clio); lyric poetry (Euterpe); tragedy (Melpomene); dance (Terpsichore); love poetry (Erato); hymns (Polyhymnia); astronomy (Urania); and comedy (Thalia)
● Roman name: Muses

The Muses

Hephaestus
■ Ancient Greeks

* ☀ Son of Zeus and Hera; Hephaestus rhymes with 'chef iced us'
* ☀ The god of blacksmiths and craftsmen
* ☀ Makes weapons for the gods on Mount Olympus

When I was born with a shrivelled foot, Hera tossed me over the cliffs of Olympus, hoping that would be my end. Instead, I plummeted through the sky for nine days and nights until I fell into the sea. The sea nymphs Eurynome and Thetis took me in and raised me in their undersea grotto. It was there that I learnt my mystical art of metalworking.

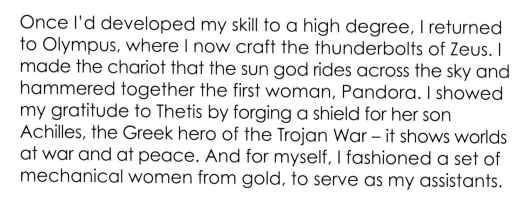

Once I'd developed my skill to a high degree, I returned to Olympus, where I now craft the thunderbolts of Zeus. I made the chariot that the sun god rides across the sky and hammered together the first woman, Pandora. I showed my gratitude to Thetis by forging a shield for her son Achilles, the Greek hero of the Trojan War – it shows worlds at war and at peace. And for myself, I fashioned a set of mechanical women from gold, to serve as my assistants.

* ● Hephaestus's symbols were the anvil, hammer and tongs
* ● On falling from Olympus, he landed on the volcanic island of Lemnos
* ● Through his association with Lemnos, he was also god of fire and volcanoes
* ● Roman name: Vulcan

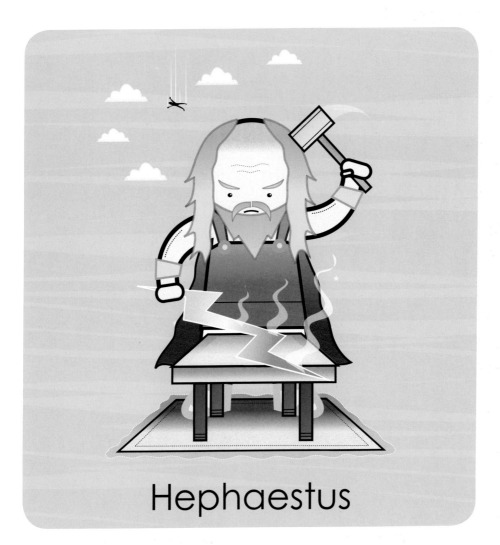

Hephaestus

Heracles
Ancient Greeks

☀ A demigod and hero; Heracles rhymes with 'expertise'
☀ The son of Zeus and mortal Alcmene
☀ Heracles is symbolized by a lion skin and a wooden club

I was born with the gift of strength that has never been equalled, and boy, have I used it! Throughout my life, my great foe Hera has hated me because Zeus is my father.

When I was an infant, Hera sent two great serpents to slay my brother and I in our crib, but I strangled those stupendous slitherers. When I married Megara, Hera drove me insane, and I killed my children in my madness. To atone, I faced 12 punishing labours. Muck out the Augean stables in one day? Sure, except they housed thousands of cattle and hadn't been cleaned in decades. No hose would do the job; instead, I diverted two mighty rivers to flow through the barn! And that was just one labour. Is it any wonder that I have given my name to tasks of unimaginable difficulty: Herculean!

● One of the labours was to capture Cerberus, guard dog of the underworld
● Heracles completed his 12 labours successfully, so he gained immortality
● On dying, the immortal part of him rose to Olympus, where he married Hebe
● Roman name: Hercules

Heracles

Odysseus
■ Ancient Greeks

✹ King of Ithaca; Odysseus rhymes with 'oblivious'
✹ Famed for his great resourcefulness, rather than his strength
✹ Best known for his difficult journey home from Troy

'Honey, I'm home!' Three simple words I thought I'd never get to say. I even tried not to leave Ithaca in the first place! I acted crazy by sowing my fields with salt, but Palamedes tossed my infant son in front of the plough. I stopped, of course, and that proved my sanity.

Little did I know my baby son would be 20 years old when I next saw him. Thanks to my wily Trojan horse trick, we Greeks finally won the war, and I set out for home. But, because of Poseidon's unreasonable hatred, the journey took me ten eventful years. I visited the island of the Lotus Eaters and later had to be lashed to the mast of my ship to resist the enchanting call of those lovely bird-women, the Sirens. I even spent a relaxing seven-year spell on the magic isle of the nymph Calypso.

● A favourite of Athena, who counselled him during his troubled journey home
● Odysseus angered Poseidon by blinding his Cyclops son, Polyphemus
● Even today, the word 'odyssey' means a long, troubled journey
● Roman name: Ulysses

Odysseus

Orpheus
Ancient Greeks

☀ Musician and poet; Orpheus rhymes with 'glorious'
☀ One of the Argonauts, Jason's great adventurers
☀ He used his lyre-playing to enchant one and all

A legendary 'rock god', when I struck a riff on my lyre, I charmed the trees out of the woods, the rivers from their courses and even persuaded Cerberus, the hound of Hades, to abandon his post as guard of the gates of hell.

I braved the dark journey to the underworld to find my wife, Eurydice. Hades claimed her after she was bitten by a viper. Using my trusty lyre, I believed I could win her back from death itself. Sure enough, Hades became my biggest fan. He agreed I could lead Eurydice up the hard road out of Hades – so long as I didn't look back. I could just see the light of the upper world when – uh oh! – I turned to smile. I saw my love fall back down to the underworld. After that loss, my death – being torn to pieces by the Maenads – was a relief. Now I can join my dearest.

● Orpheus was the son of Calliope, the Muse of epic poetry
● Some say his father was Apollo; others, a Thracian prince
● Hades was said to weep iron tears when Orpheus played his lyre
● Roman name: Orpheus

Orpheus

Medusa
Ancient Greeks

✸ One of three Gorgon sisters; Medusa rhymes with 'producer'
✸ Her hair is a tangled nest of writhing, venomous snakes
✸ Her head turns people to stone, even when severed

If you've ever been frozen to your seat by a teacher's stony glare, you have an inkling of the force that my sinister gaze holds. Mine is a face with the power to petrify: I turn men to cold, hard stone with one look.

I was born a Gorgon, daughter of the deep undersea god Phorcys. My dangerous reputation was irresistible to a proud hero with something to prove – Perseus. Even with Olympian aid from Hephaestus and Athena, it took some smart gear to kill me – a magic sword from him and a polished shield from her. Athena advised Perseus to use her shield as a mirror, so he did not have to look directly at me when he sliced off my head with the sword. From the blood spilled at my beheading, up reared the magic winged horse, Pegasus.

● Medusa was the only one of the Gorgon sisters who was mortal
● After killing her, Perseus kept her head and used it as a weapon
● Images of Medusa's head were thought to avert evil
● Roman name: Medusa

Medusa

Minotaur
Ancient Greeks

✸ Half-man, half-bull; Minotaur rhymes with 'dinosaur'
✸ The offspring of King Minos's wife, Pasiphae, and a bull
✸ Theseus kills the Minotaur using his bare hands

Is every man – or woman – part monster? That's a question King Minos of Crete didn't want to answer! When his queen, Pasiphae, gave birth to me, they hid me deep in the heart of a labyrinth. The maze was so complex that even its creator, Daedalus, had trouble finding the exit.

There I stayed, a savage beast who was fed every seven years with seven young men and seven young women. Theseus finally arrived to put me out of my misery. Minos's daughter Ariadne loved the hero and helped him. She held on to the string he unravelled on his zigzag route to my den, enabling him to retrace his steps and escape. It might astonish you to hear that Theseus abandoned his saviour Ariadne on his journey home. It doesn't surprise me, though! I'm used to the twisted, tortured ways of men.

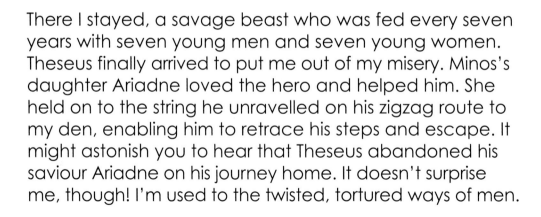

● The Minotaur's father, a beautiful white bull, had been a gift from Poseidon
● Minos dishonoured Poseidon by refusing to offer the bull in sacrifice
● Poseidon punished Minos by making Queen Pasiphae fall in love with the bull
● Roman name: Minotaurus

Minotaur

Chapter 2
Norse Legends

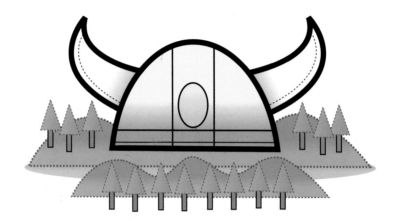

Like the bleak winter skies, shadowy pine forests and icy seas that make up the northern landscape, these stories are sombre. They tell the sorry tales of two great clans of gods – the Aesir and the Vanir – who once fought, but are now reconciled under the Aesir god Odin. He is not a shining idol, but a wizened, one-eyed man, whose folk are busy defending their homeland, Asgard. And their foe? Why, the frost giants who represent the forces of chaos. Sadly, destruction is inevitable, and these gods know it. At Ragnarok, they will die – fighting heroically in the face of their own fated doom. Where did it all go so wrong?

Odin

Yggdrasil

Bifrost

Heimdall

Thor

Sif

Loki

Hel

Balder

Tyr

Njord

Freya

Freyr

Skadi

Bragi

Gefjon

Ragnarok

Odin
Norse Legends

☀ The chief Aesir god; Odin rhymes with 'no win'
☀ Depicted as an elderly, bearded, one-eyed man
☀ His spear, Gungnir (Swaying One), never misses its mark

The god of battle, I am known for my love of war. My high-ceilinged hall, Valhalla, is crowded with my precious companions – warriors slain in my name. My throne is raised so high that I can see over all the nine known worlds.

I sacrificed one of my eyes to become wise – plucked it right out as the price to pay for a drink from Mimir's well of knowledge. And I lashed myself to Yggdrasil, the world tree, hanging exposed to the wind for nine days to obtain a vision of the future. My two ravens Huginn (Thought) and Muninn (Memory) wing their way around the nine worlds and return to caw the latest tidings from faraway places into my ear. My beloved pet wolves, Geri and Freki, skulk at the foot of my throne. I stroke their ears and think sadly of Ragnarok, the doom of the gods that I foresee will come.

● Sleipnir (Old Slippy), Odin's excellent horse, had eight legs
● At Ragnarok, Odin's men will rally to fight the giants in one final battle
● Odin is associated with Wednesday (Old Norse: odinsdagr)

Odin

Yggdrasil

■ Norse Legends

✳ Aka the world tree; Yggdrasil rhymes with 'big Brazil'
✳ The assembly point for the gods and their governing court
✳ It is described by Odin as the most noble of all trees

I am an ash tree so huge that no hurricane blast has a chance of bringing me down. I'm also party central. Beneath my big leafy top, the party of life is in full swing. The entire Norse cosmos is tangled in my branches and nourished by my three great taproots.

My branches shelter heaven and earth. My taproots meander through three worlds – the world of the Aesir gods, the world of the giants (Jotunheim) and even into the realm of the dead. Mimir's spring of knowledge burbles near my root in Jotunheim. I have an obnoxious squirrel in residence, Ratotosk (Drill Tooth), who scampers up and down my immense trunk. He spreads gossip between the eagle who teeters in my topmost branches and Nidhogg, the scaly dragon who chews on my roots.

● Yggdrasil means 'Odin's horse', which may refer to when Odin tied himself to it
● Three fates, known as the Norns, watered Yggdrasil each day
● As Ragnarok approaches, Yggdrasil's great trunk will shudder, sway and creak

Yggdrasil

Bifrost
Norse Legends

✳ A burning bridge; Bifrost rhymes with 'high cost'
✳ Spans the border of earthly Midgard and heavenly Asgard
✳ It is reserved exclusively for the use of the gods

Greetings from Asgard, realm of the gods! I'm the place where the coolest gods hang out. Standing in their stirrups, they gallop their horses across me each day – no wonder my name means 'trembling path'! They're on their way to the daily *thing* (that's Norse for council).

I'm built of three elements: green water, blue air and red fire. Call me a rainbow if you must (true, I shimmer in the sun), but I'm *not* just a pretty face! My arc of flaming colours keeps out the riff-raff – uninvited, scruffy giants, to be precise! My elemental heat keeps the sacred streams below me at boiling point. Wouldn't you know that Thor insists on wading through the scalding water each day on his way to the meeting, instead of riding across me like all the other gods? Wow, he's one tough dude!

● Bifrost was sometimes known as 'the powers' way'
● Heimdall's hall was close to Bifrost so that he could guard Asgard
● At Ragnarok, Bifrost will shatter into bits as the gods ride over it towards battle

Bifrost

Heimdall
Norse Legends

✺ Aesir watchman; Heimdall rhymes with 'same doll'
✺ His name means 'he who lights the world'
✺ He is associated with daybreak

I'm the gods' early warning system, razor-sharp and radar-equipped! Well, organic radar, if you like. I can hear grass growing, the wool thickening on sheep and Loki turning into a mosquito. And I never switch off!

I can see further than 14 kilometres, even in the dark. During the day that's useful, but at night? You try getting to sleep when one glance out the window shows what's happening on the other side of town! I prowl around Bifrost – no frost giant gets a frozen toe on it when I'm on duty. I'm there on my horse Gulltop, saving spaces for the gods to tie up their horses. I direct traffic by blasting my supersonic horn, Gjallarhorn, heard through the nine worlds. 'You there! Make way for Odin who's about to gallop up on his trusty mount, Sleipnir!'

● Heimdall's hall, Himinbjorg, means 'cliffs of heaven'
● The name refers to its location near Bifrost and the border of Asgard
● At Ragnarok, Heimdall will blow Gjallarhorn to summon the gods to combat

Heimdall

Thor
Norse Legends

☀ Aesir god and son of Odin; Thor rhymes with 'sore'
☀ The god of thunder, lightning and storms
☀ He uses his awesome tools to serve and protect the gods

Let's face it: with a name like Thor (Thunder), was I going to be the god of spring blossoms and soothing breezes? Not likely! My fiery red beard and carved stone hammer basically say: 'Frost giants, approach at your own risk!'

I'm a one-man hardware shop with some truly excellent tools. Mjolnir, my hammer, shatters rocks better than any pneumatic drill. I have to wear fireproof gloves because the force behind my fling makes Mjolnir searingly hot! I've taken my wily sidekick Loki on many of my adventures. Once he made me dress as Freya in a wedding gown and veil – a little plot to recover Mjolnir, which had been stolen by a frost giant who wanted to marry Freya. Peeking coyly from behind my veil, I reclaimed my hammer, then laid waste to the wedding party.

● Thrudvang (Power Field) was Thor's home region and Bilskirnir (Lightning Crack) his hall
● His chariot was led by two goats, Tanngrisnir (Snarler) and Tanngnjostr (Teeth Grinder)
● Thor is associated with Thursday (Old Norse: *thorsdagr*)

Thor

Sif
Norse Legends

* Thor's wife and goddess of fertility; Sif rhymes with 'whiff'
* Through association with the harvest, she stands for prosperity
* In old Norse, Sif's name means 'wife' or 'bride'

When I toss back my rich golden hair and it gently waves down my back, it's not just me being vain. You see, I wear the fate of the grain harvest on my head!

The reddish gold is the exact colour of ripening grain, and the waves imitate the wind blowing gently through a field of sheaves ready to harvest. At least, Thor always saw it that way. My life was a succession of good hair days, which meant plenty of ripe grain… until Loki caught me napping and shaved my head just for fun. Thor was not amused. He collared Loki and insisted he solve the problem – pronto! Loki turned to the crafty dwarves, who spun me a wig of gold thread that rippled in the wind and grew like real hair – or real grain. Thor was happy and the harvest saved, but I'm still stuck wearing a silly wig!

● Sif was the mother of Ull, god of archery and skiing
● Her daughter Thrud was the goddess of heathland, willows and grass
● Sif was associated with the rowan tree, which protected against witches

Sif

Loki
■ Norse Legends

✳ Thor's foster-brother and god of fire; Loki rhymes with 'pokey'
✳ Father of three evil beings: Hel, Fenrir and Jormungandr
✳ Loki gets bored easily, and when he does, watch out!

Just like the leaping flames that I represent, I can change shape in an instant. Turning into a mare one time, I gave birth to Odin's eight-legged horse Sleipnir, a steed who canters through earth, sea and sky with ease.

I warm with my cunning intelligence, but also scald with my fiendish pranks. And I can't help being mean! I was born when my father, a giant named Farbauti (Cruel Striker), struck my mother, the giantess Laufey, with a lightning bolt. Maybe that's why I'm such a demon? My tricks turned to tragedy when Balder was stabbed by a deadly dart of mistletoe thrown by his blind brother Hoder in a foolish game. I knew that mistletoe was the only thing in nature with the power to harm Balder and yet I guided Hoder's hand. What made me do it?

● Loki's boredom often got him into trouble
● He started as a champion of the gods, but his tricks made them turn on him
● At Ragnarok, Loki will lead the giants in battle against the gods

Loki

Hel
■ Norse Legends

✳ Daughter of Loki and an Aesir enemy; Hel rhymes with 'sail'
✳ Sister of the wolf Fenrir and the serpent Jormungandr
✳ She has a bowl called Hunger and a knife called Famine

Oh yeah, I'm a wreck. My face is still sort of fresh, but I have the legs of a corpse – my skin is way beyond being rescued by moisturizers, kids. Sunblock isn't necessary though because I live in Hel, far from any UV rays!

It's really grim here. I get the dreariest dead – the sick, senile and sinister ones that Odin turns away from Valhalla. There are no battle heroes in this non-stop Hallowe'en hoedown! And I can't expect any help from my good-for-nothing family, either. Two of those losers (my dad Loki and my brother, the savage wolf Fenrir) are chained to rocks, while that snake (really) Jormungandr is wrapped around the world, biting his own tail. You see how I grew up? Have some sympathy – at least I have a job and I'm trying to make a go of it!

● Odin condemned Hel to take care of the old and sick who were sent to her
● The threshold of the region Hel was known as 'stumbling block'
● At Ragnarok, all of Hel's people will accompany Loki to fight against the Aesir

Hel

Balder

Norse Legends

☀ Odin's son, god of light; Balder rhymes with 'alder'
☀ He is disturbed by dreams in which he dies
☀ Following his death, his ship becomes his funeral pyre

I was the shining, spotless god. No one had a bad word to say about me, and in a world of braggart warriors, I always spoke kindly of others. My longship *Hringhorni* was the finest of them all. But I dreamt of death – my own.

Troubled that my dreams would come true, my mother Frigg trudged through the nine worlds making every single thing that existed swear an oath to do me no harm… but it was a massive job and she grew weary and missed one small plant. Always good-natured, I let the gods goof around, bouncing rocks and spears off my body – after all, nothing could do *me* harm! But one forgotten plant and one snivelling god – jealous of my purity – spelled my doom. Thanks to Loki's trickery, I was speared through the heart by a twig of mistletoe.

● Breidablik (broad, shining) was Balder's hall; nothing unclean could enter there
● Loki tricked Balder's brother Hoder into throwing the fatal mistletoe spear
● Balder's wife Nanna died of grief and was laid in the funeral ship with him

Balder

Tyr
Norse Legends

※ An Aesir god; Tyr rhymes with 'fear'
※ A sword god and the god of justice
※ The only god brave enough to feed Fenrir (Loki's wolf son)

I often think back to that day when I laid my right hand inside the slavering fangs of the biggest, baddest wolf ever. The other gods just laughed when Fenrir snapped off my hand – they are used to carnage, after all.

The gods were afraid of Fenrir because he was destined to kill Odin. I helped them to chain him up. 'Show us how strong you are', we said. 'Break this chain!' We said we'd free him if he failed. I agreed to put my hand in his mouth. Was it as a sign of trust – or as a sacrifice because I knew we were cheating Fenrir? The chain was enchanted, forged by dwarves from impossible things like the sound of a cat's paw and a bird's spit. That wicked wolf could not break its magic spell, so he had to stay fettered. In his rage, he bit off my hand. That's justice, I guess.

● The gods chained Fenrir when he became a threat to Odin
● Gleipnir was the name of the chain used to fetter Fenrir
● Tyr is associated with Tuesday (Old Norse: *tysdagr*)

Tyr

Njord
■ Norse Legends

☀ Vanir god of prosperity; Njord rhymes with 'fjord'
☀ Father to Freya and Freyr with the mother goddess, Nerthus
☀ God of seafaring and fishing, good winds and summer seas

When Skadi demanded a godly husband as compensation for the slaying of her father, the frost giant Thiassi, Odin made us all line up behind a curtain. Skadi could choose the feet that made her heart flutter fastest, he said – and my toes were just too darn cute to turn down!

Maybe it was all those organic sea-salt soaks that made my soles the standouts? True, Skadi was disappointed when she discovered I wasn't Balder (between you and me, the 'white god' has pale, pasty feet), but a deal is a deal. We married, but it didn't work out. I missed the honking of my swans in secluded sea coves and she hankered for the howls of wolves in her land of giants so now we live apart. I keep busy calming the waters so that the sea folk I support can make a decent living.

● A diplomat, he lived with the Aesir to cement their peace with the Vanir
● Njord's home Noatun means 'enclosure of ships' or 'anchorage'
● After Ragnarok, Njord is fated to survive and return to the Vanir

Njord

Freya
Norse Legends

☀ Freyr's sister, goddess of fertility; Freya rhymes with 'layer'
☀ Wears a falcon-feather cloak and has a cat-drawn chariot
☀ Owns Brisingamen, a necklace of lacy gold studded with gems

I'm head of the Valkyries, the ladies who keep track of the heroic dead during battle. I direct the slain to Sessrumnir, my hall, where I offer an afterlife of rest and relaxation. True, I'm in competition with Odin and Valhalla, but some of the guys prefer an afterlife with me. Unlike Odin, I have *two* eyes, and I don't allow wolves or ravens in the dining hall.

Freya

● Freya's husband Odr was often away and she wept tears of pure gold for him
● When she went to search for him, winter came; when she returned, it was spring
● Freya is associated with Friday (Old Norse: *frjadagr*)

Freyr

Norse Legends

* ☀ Njord's son, prince of the Vanir; Freyr rhymes with 'lair'
* ☀ He is angered if blood is spilled near his fertile fields
* ☀ His pet boar has golden bristles, symbolizing the sun's rays

Freyr

Prince, warrior, lover. Warrior? It's a must in my culture. At heart, though, I'm a lover. I bring my subjects sunshine and prosperity. Fantastic presents always seem to come my way. Let me show you my excellent longship, *Skidbladnir* – dwarf-made, naturally. See, it's big enough for all the gods, but folds up into this little pouch. Neat, eh?

* ● When Freyr pined for the giantess Gerda, he sent his servant Skirnir to woo her
* ● Skirnir demanded Freyr's self-fighting sword as payment
* ● At Ragnarok, swordless Freyr will have to fight the giant Beli with a deer antler

Skadi

Norse Legends

* Goddess of winter and the hunt; Skadi rhymes with 'baddy'
* A giant, her name is related to the Saxon word for 'shadow'
* She marries Njord, father of Freya and Freyr

Picture my life. I'm at home in a shadowy pine forest, a giant cross-country skier who demolishes hills in a few long strides. A single twang of my bow string and I've brought down my own wild dinner. I wake at midnight to wolf song. My life is independent, but sometimes I just need a bit of fun. That's when I turn to the gods.

I went visiting – armed with my bow – to avenge my father, Thiassi. The gods offered me gold, but I asked for a husband and challenged them to make me laugh. I admit I did smile when I saw their slightly stinky line-up of godly clodhoppers. I chose the one with the cutest feet, hoping it would be Balder, but no, I'd picked salty old Njord! Our marriage only lasted nine days, but I returned to my homeland with no hard feelings.

- Skadi's father was slain as punishment for stealing Idun's apples of youth
- Odin tossed Thiassi's eyes into the night sky where they became stars
- Skadi complained of the screeching gulls in Njord's seaside homeland

Skadi

Bragi
■ Norse Legends

✳ Son of Odin, god of poetry; Bragi rhymes with 'vaguely'
✳ A giant, he was born in a cave of glittering stalactites
✳ Married to Idun, goddess of eternal youth

So you think texting is cool? To a guy with runes tattooed on his tongue, that is *sooo* boring! I take the spoken word (skaldic poetry, that is) super-seriously. I have a gift for it.

There is no Twitter here. To broadcast our latest deeds of derring-do, we need skalds (poets) like me. I just stand up at the banqueting table, toss my long beard over my shoulder to keep it out of the mead (there's nothing like the mead of poetry to bring on inspiration), and start bragging about brave acts. I'm also associated with oaths – the kind you use to swear a solemn promise. A swig of the mead of poetry, anyone? We pass the goblet around and swear to the important stuff, like supporting Odin in coming battles, remembering fallen warriors and giving thanks to Freyr and Freya for good harvests.

● Gunnlod guarded the sacred mead of poetry in the cave in which Bragi was born
● Odin wanted the mead for himself, so he entered the cave as a serpent
● Odin and Gunnlod bartered for the mead, and Odin fathered Bragi

Bragi

Gefjon
Norse Legends

✳ An Aesir, goddess of ploughing; Gefjon rhymes with 'Teflon'
✳ Wife of Skjöld, king of the Danes and son of Odin
✳ She is associated with good luck and virtue

It takes a special kind of woman to be a goddess – one who's willing to turn her four sons into oxen and hitch them to a plough. Oh, they bellowed alright, but I just cracked my whip. 'Yahhh! Move on boys – I mean, team!'

You see, in exchange for my hospitality, King Gylfi offered me as much land in his kingdom as I could plough in one day and one night. What he didn't know is that I'm an Aesir and a goddess! How could I turn down such a sweet real-estate deal? So I just zapped my boys into oxen (they were giants anyway, so size wasn't an issue) and we set to work. The boys really got into it! They didn't just plough though, they uprooted an entire peninsula! So, I tossed it into the sea as a bit of extra farmland for us. Today, it's the Danish island of Zealand.

● Gefjon's name translates as 'giver'
● A statue in Copenhagen, Denmark, shows Gefjon cracking the whip over her bulls
● The hole created by the ploughing became the Swedish Lake Mälaren

Gefjon

Ragnarok
Norse Legends

✳ The doom of the gods; Ragnarok rhymes with 'aftershock'
✳ Ends in the final battle between the Aesir and their enemies
✳ Foreseen by Odin, the god of battle

Those Norse gods may love a good fight, but when I arrive, I'm taking battle to the next level! I plan to sweep in, bringing doom to the max. It's the end of the world – time for Loki's children, Fenrir and Jormungandr, to have their vengeance. Scary, or what?

None of this has happened yet, but it will. It's in the runes! First Heimdall blows his great horn to call the gods to battle! Next, mighty Yggdrasil's trunk shudders violently. Then it's on to the vast plain of Vigrid (aka the Battle Shaker), for the fated finale. Even Odin and his spear perish – sucked into the gaping mouth of my wolf-pal Fenrir. Brave Thor does his best, heaving his hammer Mjolnir in a mighty blow that shatters Jormungandr's head. But that spells curtains for Thor. Time's up, guys!

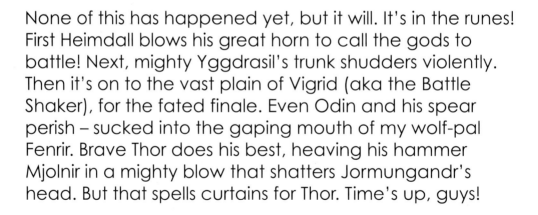

● Fenrir the wolf had yawning jaws that touched the earth and the sky
● Jormungandr was a serpent who was trying to squish the world
● Thor drowned in venom that spewed from Jormungandr's crushed fangs

Ragnarok

Chapter 3
Egyptian Divinities

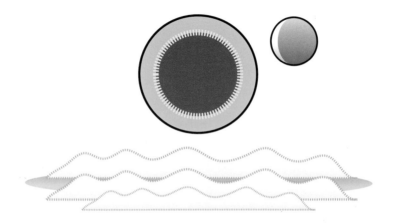

Beaks, snouts and sky-spanning wings... Vulture crowns and cobra headdresses... Face it, these guys are out there. They put their best sides forward and, yes, it's a bit like a zoo at times, but that's just how it is! Maybe it's their close connection to the harsh climate in the Egyptian homeland that makes this lot so extreme. Flowing through their story is the Nile river, providing water for irrigation and fertile mud on the fields during flood time. When the floods don't come, the land dries up and life withers. No wonder these stories are of gods who can prowl the desert in jackal form or soar over the burning sands as a falcon.

Bennu Bird

Ra

Mut

Nut

Osiris

Isis

Horus

Hathor

Seth

Nephthys

Anubis

Thoth

Seshat

Sekhmet

Ptah

Bastet

Bes

Sobek

Rameses II

Bennu Bird
Egyptian Divinities

☀ This bird symbolizes creation; Bennu rhymes with 'hey you'
☀ 'Bennu' means to rise and shine
☀ Represents the *ba*, or essential being, of the sun god

I was the third thing. First came the primeval, chaotic swirl of waters known as the Nun. Next, a plain mound – the Benben Stone – rose from the bottomless depth of the water. Then me! The Benben Stone was there waiting for me at the beginning of time, so I arrived to perch on it.

I touched down on the stone, lifted my fluttering wings and opened my beak to give one croaky cry. The first sound in the new world! A squawk, really. Its vibrations rippled the surface of the water, creating change in time. 'Begin!' That is what my cry said. 'Let the world begin!' True to my name, I was telling the world it was time to rise and shine! And me, where did I come from? Who were my parents? Well, my name also means 'he who came into being by himself'. Some things just are.

● The chaotic waters (the Nun) were all that existed before creation
● The Benben Stone was an oval stone that arose from the Nun
● It represented the heaps of fertile silt left after Nile flood waters receded

Bennu Bird

Ra
Egyptian Divinities

✴ The sun god and source of all life; Ra rhymes with 'ah'
✴ The sky goddess Nut is said to swallow him at night
✴ Nut then gives birth to him again each morning

Ah, cruising those colour-splashed skies as I begin to rise at dawn. Just my bros and I in the *Mesektet* – my awesome night barque – it doesn't get better than that!

My wild night spent dodging danger (in fact, the serpent Apophis) in Duat, the underworld, is just about over. I'm ready to hop on my day ride, the solar barque known as the *Mandjet*. I grab my solar disk and settle it into the centre of my crown, the better to attract the worship of my loyal subjects. They're trudging toward the wheat and barley fields, wiping their sweaty brows in relief. Once again I, Ra, sun god supreme, have conquered the forces of night chaos and returned. 'Yo! It's me, Ra, ready to bring light, life and food to the Nile valley, sailing at full tilt across the sky in my daily royal procession'.

● At midday, Ra is portrayed with a hawk's head topped by the solar disk
● He has the head of a human in the evening, and that of a ram at night
● In the morning, Ra is depicted with the head of a scarab beetle

Ra

Mut
Egyptian Divinities

✳ The queen-mother goddess; Mut rhymes with 'scoot'
✳ Her name comes from the Egyptian word for 'mother'
✳ Mut, Amun and Khonsu are known as the triad of Thebes

A respectable and settled matron, I am the consort of the king of the gods, Amun-Ra, and mother to the moon god Khonsu. I also happen to be a wily politician.

I use my matriarchal influence to keep father–son rivalry in check. Thanks to me, the sun and moon rise and set on schedule, the tides are predictable, the Nile floods so that crops can grow – and everybody gets to eat! Like so many mature ladies, I adore feathered hats. My favourite is a large vulture set into a crown that drapes stylishly over my head. In Egypt, vultures symbolize motherhood. When I married Amun, I insisted we move to Thebes, where I promoted an alliance with Ra (creating a whole new god, Amun-Ra). I even demanded a new temple – and got one – the delightful Karnak.

● Mut usually held the Was Sceptre, a symbol of dominion
● She was the only goddess portrayed wearing the double crown of Egypt
● The double crown emphasized her role in unifying Upper and Lower Egypt

Mut

Nut
Egyptian Divinities

✴ A sky goddess; Nut rhymes with 'shoot'
✴ Daughter of Shu, god of air, and Tefnut, goddess of moisture
✴ The mother of Osiris, Isis, Seth and Nephthys

Core strength? Baby, I've got it! How else do you think I've stayed balanced on my tippy-toes for thousands of years, with my back in this extreme arch forming the sky?

My body is truly heavenly: it's speckled with a multitude of stars that represent the worthy dead. Way back, my earthy consort Geb and I nestled so close together that nothing could grow between us. Bossy Shu gave me a sharp poke in the belly that sent me up, up and away from him. I became a fixed celestial firmament and gave birth to Osiris, Isis, Seth and Nephthys. My separation from Geb created a sky like a sea for Ra to sail along each day. At night I swallow that swashbuckler only to give birth to him again every dawn. Poor Geb didn't take our split well, though: he shook so hard that he created earthquakes!

● Nut was especially associated with the night sky and the Milky Way
● Red sky at dawn was thought to be the blood of Nut giving birth to Ra
● Her image was painted on coffin lids so that she could embrace the dead

Nut

Osiris
Egyptian Divinities

☀ Son of Geb and Nut; Osiris rhymes with 'oh wire us'
☀ Usually shown as a green man with mummy-bandaged legs
☀ He wears the Atef crown (white with two red ostrich feathers)

My career went viral after my death and I'm one busy mummy! I was living the lush life of your average universal lord and vegetation god, teaching men to bake bread and ferment wine, and acting as a just lawgiver. But then my brother Seth pulled me to pieces and scattered my remains in the desert. That guy just loves to cause trouble.

On the other hand, I never should have taken the bet and laid down in the coffin during that party. Next thing I knew, Seth slammed the lid shut, and I was at his mercy. My darling wife Isis zapped me back together with a quick spell, but I needed time to heal spiritually. Now I am king and judge of Duat, the underworld. And since I died and was reborn, I am honoured as the god who renews nature and kick-starts the annual agricultural cycle.

● Osiris reigned in the Hall of the Two Truths, overseeing the weighing of hearts
● He granted immortality to anyone whose heart balanced Maat's feather of truth
● After his resurrection by Isis, Osiris fathered Horus with her

Osiris

Isis
Egyptian Divinities

☀ Isis is Osiris's wife and sister; Isis rhymes with 'crisis'
☀ Her name means throne; she is the throne goddess
☀ She is often portrayed on a throne, nursing her son Horus

'Pull yourself together!' I chanted this simple, but effective spell over the 14 torn pieces of my husband Osiris's body when Nephthys and I eventually found him after a long search. He had been dismembered by our jealous brother, Seth... Don't you just hate sibling rivalry?

Anyway, it worked. Osiris resurrected, fathered our son Horus (the pharaoh!) and took a new job ruling the underworld. There, he could stay clear of the complicated family vibes above ground. I miss him, but I've got plenty to do here in Egypt. A lot gets sheltered, or should I say swept, under my wide wings, let me tell you. Just lifting them is a chore, but it's part of the job description – I am now a single mother working as Egypt's protectress and number one maternal goddess.

● Isis is depicted with the huge wings of a kite, a soaring bird of prey
● She gained power over Ra by tricking him into revealing his secret name
● The Romans liked Isis so much that they worshipped her, too

Isis

Horus
Egyptian Divinities

☀ The son of Osiris and Isis; Horus rhymes with 'chorus'
☀ In youth he is often portrayed with his finger in his mouth
☀ Horus has different forms; an earlier myth links him to Ra

Sometimes, when all the princely pressure on me gets too intense, I just take off and soar along on the air currents. I'm not only a prince, but also a sky god and a falcon.

Divine inheritance is never simple! After Uncle Seth murdered my dad Osiris, my mum Isis flew all over the desert looking for him. She resurrected him, but he split for the underworld. Mum raised me (in secret) so I could take revenge and restore *maat* (divine order) to Egypt. A good son, I try my best, and in the process get my eyes ripped out! (Seth is a merciless animal.) Of course, Egypt's sky goes dark, because my left eye represents the moon and my right eye the sun. (Like I said, royal genes, royal pain.) Thoth restores my eyes, and the battle royale goes on. Wish me luck.

● His conflict with Seth symbolized the rivalry between Upper and Lower Egypt
● The 'Horus Eye' is a human eye with falcon markings
● Pharaohs were considered the 'living Horus' on earth

Horus

Hathor
Egyptian Divinities

✳ Goddess of femininity; Hathor rhymes with 'maths bore'
✳ Her headdress has a red sun disk set inside cow horns
✳ She is also the goddess of music

Multitasking? Tell me about it. I have to work hard to spread my wonderfulness around. I serve as the official welcomer to the underworld. Just the sight of me makes the newly dead calm down and cheer up!

Working overtime in the underworld can be hard on the complexion, so I like to freshen up with one of the beauty potions I concoct. Then it's off to the souk, where I take my cow form so that I can eavesdrop on the progress of the romances that I am currently stage-managing. When one goes according to plan, I have to brush up on my sistrum-playing for the wedding, where I rattle it and help everyone get down. That just leaves time to get to the birth chamber, where I take turns with Tawaret to soothe the fears of women in childbirth.

● A sistrum is a percussion instrument, associated with Hathor as goddess of music
● Hathor and her priestesses were sometimes shown wearing long, red scarves
● The Greeks linked Hathor to their goddess Aphrodite

Hathor

Seth
Egyptian Divinities

✳ The chaotic opposite of Osiris; Seth rhymes with 'bet'
✳ Father (with Nephthys) of the wild jackal Anubis
✳ He is often portrayed with red hair and skin

Anteater? Aardvark? Or just a guy in serious need of a nose job? You decide! It's the battle of the super-bad beaks, the Seth animal wrestling match! Sandstorm? Flash flood? Sibling assassination? If bad stuff happens in ancient Egypt, you know I'm the god behind it.

Even my looks spell anarchy: the sickle-shaped snout, forked tail and sawn-off ears. Even though they know I killed my brother Osiris, the gods aren't too proud to call me when they need an enforcer. That's me standing in the prow of the sun barque, spearing the serpent Apophis so that Ra can sail along unharmed. Hey, brute strength has its benefits! And without me to kick around, Horus would just be Isis's baby boy. Every privileged prince needs a baddy to banish. I do what I can!

● Seth was connected with the desert of Upper Egypt (the 'red land')
● He tore out Horus's eyes during their long conflict
● Reconciliation with Horus symbolized unification of Upper and Lower Egypt

Seth

Nephthys
Egyptian Divinities

✸ Daughter of Nut; Nephthys rhymes with 'chef sees'
✸ Nephthys is sister to Isis, Osiris and Seth
✸ Her major role is mourner and protectress of the dead

Ever heard of me? No, I thought not. That's because I'm the neglected middle child in constant competition with my super-fab big sister, Isis. Yes, *that* Isis. How can I get any attention as a goddess when she's in the way?

Would you believe that there's not a single temple devoted to me and only me? Blimey! When there's a job nobody wants, guess who gets it? Marriage to that beast Seth? Nephthys won't mind! Goddess of the bandages that wrap mummies? Yup, me. In fact, they are known as the 'tresses of Nephthys'. Thank you *so* much! Still, I can't help but be loyal and devoted to Isis – she does that to you. I was there for her at her biggest crisis – together we searched for Osiris's body and we both took the form of kites to mourn him. When Isis resurrected him, I washed the body.

● Unlike Isis, Nephthys did not have a cult following
● Egyptian professional mourners were called 'the kites of Nephthys'
● With three others, she guarded the corners of a pharaoh's sarcophagus

Nephthys

Anubis
Egyptian Divinities

✳ Son of Nephthys and Osiris; Anubis rhymes with 'a new kiss'
✳ Nephthys abandoned him as a baby, but Isis rescued him
✳ He is usually portrayed as a black jackal

Just who are you calling a dog? I'm a wild jackal! I was first noticed prowling the edges of cemeteries, and the early Egyptians were scared I'd eat the corpses. Not a good thing, because they believed bodies needed to be preserved so they could live after death!

To keep me happy and distract my scavenger's hunger, they gave me a job as the god of embalming. I got so good at it, I even mummified Osiris's body for Isis. And like all dogs, I'm a good guard. That's why the Egyptians carved my image at the entrance to tombs, ready to take a bite out of anyone daring to rob them! True to my canine roots, I also lead men when they need it most, showing them the way through the underworld as they head to Osiris to receive their judgment.

● Anubis performed the weighing of hearts for the presiding god Osiris
● He was known as 'the dog who swallowed millions'
● Embalmers wore jackal masks during ceremonies to re-animate the dead

Anubis

Thoth
Egyptian Divinities

✳ God of writing and secret knowledge; Thoth rhymes with 'both'
✳ He often acts as a problem solver for gods in trouble
✳ Usually portrayed as a man with the head of an ibis

Scribe to the gods, I'm the guy who handles hieroglyphs. Forget smartphones – I'm talking reed, ink palette and papyrus. I may look like an ibis, but I'm no birdbrain – crisis management is my speciality. When young Horus lopped off his mum Isis's head, I'm the guy who found her a new one – a cow's! Well, I had a lot on that day...

Thoth

● An ibis is a bird with a sickle-shaped beak
● Thoth kept order, enforcing the law of *maat* (divine order)
● The *Book of Thoth* is said to contain 42 texts of occult (magic) knowledge

Seshat

Egyptian Divinities

☀ Daughter or consort of Thoth; Seshat rhymes with 'thresh at'
☀ She is known as 'foremost in the library'
☀ Her headdress is a seven-pointed plant that may be papyrus

Seshat

Known for my slinky, feline pelt, I'm goddess of maths, measuring, record-keeping, building, astronomy and libraries. I supervise when the tape measure is marking out building foundations. That way their sacred dimensions are always in accord with the moon and stars. How else could the pyramids have lasted so long, if not for my super geometry skills?

● Seshat kept the royal genealogies
● The panther skin that Seshat wore is the traditional garment of Sem priests
● The skin was usually tied at the neck by the paws

Sekhmet
Egyptian Divinities

☀ The consort of Ptah; Sekhmet rhymes with 'get set'
☀ She is portrayed as a woman with a lion's head
☀ Her crown was a sun disk with a uraeus (sacred cobra)

I'm on the rampage again! A lioness whose hot breath formed the desert, I've always been hard to control. Because I am goddess of punishment, Ra sent me down to earth to exact a little vengeance, but I had so much fun I refused to stop, and slaughtered millions. I would have carried on forever if Ra hadn't slaked my thirst with fake blood concocted of pomegranate juice and beer.

You see, blazing a path of destruction is my speciality: my roar conjures up diseases like the plague. Because my powerful magic can cause scorching high fevers and sunstroke, my priests had to learn medicine. They became skilled at healing and then the cowering humans made me goddess of medicine. More sacrifices, you scaredy-cats! That's what I am hungry for.

● Sekhmet was said to prowl the edge of the desert (the habitat of real lions)
● Pharaoh Rameses II said she rode in his chariot to destroy Egypt's enemies
● She was called 'she who dances on blood'

Sekhmet

Ptah
Egyptian Divinities

✳ 'He who is beautiful of face'; Ptah rhymes with 'ta'
✳ His skin was the blue of the sky
✳ He was the patron of craftsmen and architects

No matter how my name sounds, I'm not the Egyptian god of spit! In fact, I happen to be one very intellectual guy. By the power of my own heartfelt thought, commanded in the words of my tongue, I fashioned the world.

I am shown face forward and ramrod straight, wrapped in a tight shroud and wearing a simple skullcap on my head. My hands peek out, tightly gripping the *djed* pillar that holds up the world's ceiling. Because I built such an amazing world out of thought and words, craftsmen look to me for guidance. I use another builder's tool – the adze – to open the mouths of the mummified dead so that their senses will return. To relax, I head over to my sanctuary to visit the Apis bull. He is sacred to me and lives in palatial digs – he eats better than I do!

● Ptah's cult was based in the Egyptian city of Memphis
● Ancient Egyptians believed the heart, not the brain, was the organ of thought
● The 'opening of the mouth' ceremony symbolically revived mummies

Ptah

Bastet
Egyptian Divinities

☀ A cat goddess; Bastet rhymes with 'basket'
☀ Her ears and nose are pierced with gold rings
☀ She protects against infectious disease and evil spirits

Sleek and stylish, I find the brash, heavy weaponry of the big-boy gods quite unnecessary. My honed fangs and razor claws are quite lethal enough, thank you. Who needs a battle cry when a simple hiss will do the job?

I rid the royal granaries of rats and slay snakes that invade Egyptian homes. My battle against vermin makes me goddess of protection against disease and evil spirits. My father Ra chose me as his avenger and protectress because he knows that I'm moody and can move from purr to pounce in one swift swipe of a barbed paw. The yearly festival at my temple in Bubastis has been known throughout history as the cat's whiskers: thousands of people arrive at the temple by boat to shake sistrums, dance, feast and have a caterwauling good time!

● Originally a lioness goddess, Bastet became a domestic cat in around 900 BCE
● Bastet's name means 'she of the ointment jar'
● Ointments were used for healing

Bastet

Bes
Egyptian Divinities

☀ Protector of mothers and their children; Bes rhymes with 'mess'
☀ He is often portrayed sticking out his tongue
☀ Usually shown in a full-frontal squat rather than in side profile

Who'd you rather have hanging around the house? Horus the screeching falcon? Thoth, looking down his long sickle nose and taking notes? Or me – a happy little guy who's not afraid to look plump in a loincloth?

Everybody's favourite household god, I'm the best friend and protector of mums and babies. With my chubby cheeks and stuck-out tongue, I've been teaching my little Egyptian charges to make rude noises for centuries. Tiny but terrible, my funny, fierce face was carved on the knives used to draw enchanted circles around cots to ward off evil – and on magic wands, too. Since I'm always about, the ladies got used to asking me for beauty advice. I am often found carved on make-up jars and I'm proud to serve as the god of cosmetics!

● Ivory 'apotropaic' (to ward off evil) wands were shaped like boomerangs
● They were often engraved with images of Bes
● If a baby made a funny face, it was because 'Bes tickled him'

Bes

Sobek
Egyptian Divinities

* A Nile crocodile; Sobek rhymes with 'go check'
* Known as 'the raging one' and 'lord of the winding waterway'
* He is thought to protect against evil

These ancient Egyptians really know how to treat a reptile. We crocs go first class here – we may still lurk around in marshes, but we're worshipped for it!

For a crocodile, the perks of being divine are hard to beat. I have my own city for starters: Crocodilopolis! I live here in temples with my brothers, basking by the pool and sporting gold ankle bracelets. Yep, crocodile bling is big business here. Nile crocs even get mummified when they die. It's just one more way for the Egyptians to appease me, so I don't snap up any major body parts. I act as a bodyguard and enforcer for the pharaoh when he needs a god with fangs to turn up the terror. All I have to do is yawn wide, and the pharaoh's word is law. Evil magic? I just gobble it up – I have fabulous digestion!

● Faiyum, a marshy area in Middle Egypt, was the centre of Sobek's cult
● A necropolis (cemetery) of mummified crocodiles was found at Kom Ombo
● Death by crocodile was tragic because it left no body to live in the afterlife

Sobek

Rameses II
Egyptian Divinities

✲ Third ruler of the 19th dynasty; Rameses rhymes with 'cheese'
✲ His reign lasted 67 years (1279–1212 BCE) and he lived to 93
✲ He fought the Hittites, who invaded Egypt from the north

Name recognition! Promoting the brand! Spin! Way before the Internet age, I knew that these three things are crucial if you want to be proclaimed a god.

When I just about lost the Battle of Kadesh to the Hittites, I ignored that inconvenient truth and sent tales of victory back to Egypt. Thank Ra no reporters with smartphones were lurking! When I got back home, I spared no expense building temples like the Ramesseum, which I filled with papyrus scrolls and engraved columns describing my battle successes. And when the Hittites refused to go away, I used my good looks to marry a Hittite princess! Then I focused on establishing my legacy: 100 sons and daughters (more or less). Who knows, *you* might be related to me! I think I've earned my name – son of Ra.

● Rameses's world-famous temple is at Abu Simbel in Nubia, southern Egypt
● It has a sanctuary with statues of Ra, Ptah and Amun-Ra of Thebes
● The facade features four 20-metre high statues of Rameses

Rameses II

Roman Deities

The ancient Romans adopted many of the Greek gods and goddesses and gave them Latin names. There are several reasons for this. By the time Rome was founded, around 753 BCE, Greek civilization was already in full flower. The Italian peninsula and Greece are geographic neighbours. Thanks to Greek settlements in Italy, the Romans were familiar with the Greek stories by the time the Roman empire began to gain power over Greece.

The Romans made those Greek gods that best suited their temperament more important. For example, the Greek Ares became the Roman mega-god Mars. As god of war he was a good fit for Rome's military-based society. Later, Roman poets such as Ovid and Virgil added their own new tales about the Greek pantheon, helping Greek myth to become even more popular and to endure throughout the centuries.

Greek deities (**bold**) with their Roman equivalents

Zeus Jupiter

Hera Juno

Poseidon Neptune

Hades Pluto

Ares Mars

Hebe Juventus

Artemis Diana

Apollo Apollo

Hermes Mercury

Athena Minerva

Aphrodite Venus

Demeter Ceres

Dionysus Bacchus

Asclepius Aesculapius

Pan Faunus

Muses Muses

Hephaestus Vulcan

Heracles Hercules

Odysseus Ulysses

Orpheus Orpheus

Medusa Medusa

Minotaur Minotaurus

Index

Pages that show characters are in **bold**

Glossary

Aesir One of two clans of Norse gods (the other was the Vanir). The Aesir were associated with war and battle. Asgard was their home.

Argonauts A band of ancient Greek heroes who sailed with Jason on his ship, the *Argo*, on a quest to find the Golden Fleece.

barque A ship propelled by sails or oars, used by the ancient Egyptian god Ra.

braggart Someone who has a tendency to brag, boast or tell tall tales in order to boost his or her reputation; a show-off.

celestial An adjective that relates to the sky or the heavens. It often implies something exceedingly delightful or divinely pleasant.

consort A spouse or romantic partner, especially of a royal or divine person.

cult A religious group or system with its own rites and ceremonies.

Eleusinian Mysteries Cult ceremonies held for thousands of years at Eleusis, a town near Athens, Greece, to honour the agricultural and fertility goddess Demeter.

embalm To treat a dead body with preservatives in order to delay or prevent its decay, as used in ancient Egypt.

Fates Known as the Moirae in Greece and the Norns in Norse, these were three old women who spun out the 'thread' of a person's life and 'cut' it at the end. Even the gods submitted to them.

fertility An abundance in agricultural, human and animal reproduction, as promoted by dedicated gods.

firmament The sky. The word emphasizes the sky's vaulted shape, as a vast arch or a heavenly, cathedral-like dome.

funeral pyre A platform, usually made of wood, that a dead body is placed on to be burned during a ritual funeral rite.

Furies Also known as the Erinyes, three women who pursued and punished the evil on earth. They were known as ministers of justice.

genealogy A genetic line of descent by blood; ancestry.

hubris Behaving with excessive pride, as though equal to the gods. In Greek myth, such behaviour leads to terrible punishment.

immortal Immortal gods (like the Greek ones) live forever.

Ithaca An island in the Ionian sea, home of King Odysseus, hero of Homer's epic poem *The Odyssey*.

mead A drink made of fermented honey and water. The favoured drink of Norse gods and bards.

mortal Mortal gods (like the Norse ones) will die.

Mount Olympus The highest mountain in Greece. Believed by ancient Greeks to be the idyllic dwelling place of the gods.

nymph A minor female goddess associated with natural places such as forests, streams or rivers.

oracle A person (usually a priestess) inspired by the gods to make prophecies (predictions of events that will happen).

primeval An adjective describing something very old and primitive. Relating to a time before civilization's influence.

resurrect To restore to life from death.

runes Alphabetic characters (dating from 1 CE) that may have been used as magical charms. They feature in Norse mythology.

Glossary

sarcophagus In ancient Egypt, an exterior stone or alabaster tomb into which the wooden coffins of the very wealthy were placed. They were often painted to resemble the deceased.

Sirens Sea nymphs who lured sailors to death by drowning with their exotic singing voices. They are often shown as women with the lower bodies of birds.

souk A Middle Eastern word for a marketplace.

Stymphalian birds In Greek mythology, man-eating birds with feathers like arrows or spears and beaks like daggers.

sylvan grove A pleasant, shaded, sheltered wood, often the setting for mythic stories of ancient Greece.

Titans The 12 earliest Greek gods, children of Uranus (heavens) and Gaia (earth) and parents of the Olympian gods. Stories about the Titans are mostly about the ancestry of the Olympians.

triad An associated group of three.

Trojan War Ten-year war waged by the Greeks against the city of Troy after the Trojan prince Paris took Helen, wife of the Greek king, Menelaus. The war features in great works of literature such as Homer's *Iliad* and *Odyssey*, as well as in classic plays.

Valkyrie In Norse mythology, female goddesses who ride flying horses during battle and choose the warriors who are to be slain and taken to Valhalla.

Vanir The second of two clans of Norse deities. They lost to the Aesir in the Aesir–Vanir war. The Vanirs (Freyr, Freya and Njord) tended to be associated with fertility and the earth.